Unpromised Remedies

Index

<u>Dedication</u>

To my parents and family for supporting me in everything I do
and for acting interested everytime I told them I wrote a new
poem, my partner who is my biggest inspiration and greatest
accomplishment, my friends who've never failed to encourage
me, Mr S. Walker whose chats and immeasurable succour
interested me in poetry more so than I ever thought possible
and to those reading this who believe they're alone,
you're not.

Provoking speech

"If a tree fell in a forest and nobody's around to hear it,
would it make a sound?".
That age old phrase,
that question,
brought up many more times than it's understood.
No one really thinks to look into the phrase as it's used so often,
but its meaning and the thoughts that the phrase provokes are ineffable.

I feel like a cultivated caterpillar,
one that now has cultured into a butterfly that yet still hasn't released
itself from the isolation of its cocoon.
Imprisoned by the self deprivation of cordial life,
panicked by the thought of certainty,
threatened by the feeling of being secure.
Almost as if it's erroneous to feel protected.
Too risky to leave the impregnable desolate home,
why would anyone in their right mind exchange that character of safety
for the prospect of an endangered life.

If I scream, and nobody is around to hear it,
Do I make a sound?
If I cry does it have the same effect?
It wouldn't have to be a negative concern of course,
The same would happen if I were to laugh or grin.
What's the point in portraying an emotion if it weren't to have any effect
on others?
If you were to tell someone what was troubling you,
it wouldn't make them feel warm or at home,
it'd cause them to be distressed and urged to help even if they feel they
can't.
That would be an effect on someone else but would that make me an
atrocious person,
that I would willingly misuse someone's kindness,
that I would disservice a friend's feelings inevitably for the gratitude of
my own.

4

I feel the world's poisonous symphony of emotions paired with the self
built poison I indulge myself in is digesting my every thought,
gatekeeping it,
causing it to be inaccessible.
All I can wish for is peace.
The sweet release I so yearn for, the release of the destructive cord I'm
holding myself on.
I simply cannot bring myself to withdraw from my 'cocoon'.
It wouldn't be fair on myself or the community around me.

For now I remain quiet,
I can't truly be imprisoned if it's willing.
I put on another smile for another day,
one that keeps people from questioning the thought behind my eyes.
"If a tree fell in a forest and nobody's around to hear it, would it make a
sound?"...
Well that inescapably falls upon if the tree found it necessary to make a
sound.
To cause a commotion for a pessimistic result.
To start a riot over something that was always apprehended to harm.

Unrequited love

It's said that love at first sight is always a mutual thing,
I beg to differ.
If you believe that,
then you surely haven't been through the pain of seeing that person
everyday,
wanting to whisper sweet sentiments into their ears.
To bless their lips with a kiss as soft as satin,
 yet having to simply just smile or nod.

The excruciating suffering of acting like everything's normal between you
and them,
having to act,
as if you aren't infatuated with every word that they delicately release
from their lips.
Having to pretend you don't go out of your way for conversations with
them,
that you don't walk the same route every day,
purely as there's a slim chance of seeing them on that very route.

It's a burden,
one that's carried with you through thick and thin,
as you're too frightened to lose this person,
Ruin the little blessings you have with them,
which to you, means the world.
There's no jeopardising your simple companionship for a fortunate
stroke of serendipity.
That isn't an option for a fool in love.

The thorns of a rose

Why, if you see I'm hurt,
Do you hesitate to even attempt to help?
I love you,
Those words will forever hold meaning to us,
Yet how come you tease me with your love?
Why is it that you make me love sick,
But I simply make you sick.
No one likes a tease,
Yet I love one.
You; key to my locked heart,
You; guard of the lock.

"All's fair in love and war"

The screams,
The sirens,
No silence.
Bombs away,
The sound of dropping missiles,
The sacrifice it took and carries on taking.
When will it end?
When will we be fulfilled of the promised co-existence,
Will we ever be unrestrained to even simply solitarily exist.

Where has the daylight gone,
it's incredibly missed.
When can we go outside again?
It's all I could wish.
What have us people of the world done to deserve this?
Who has put this hell on earth upon us,
It must be a work of lucifer, this terrifying crisis.
Why does the devil find it necessary to gift us his unrelenting kiss.
How could anyone look at war and see it to hold any bliss.

The ballerina

1-and 2, 3; 1, 2, 3, 4;
I float when I dance.
1 and a 2 and a 3,
I find peace in the melody.
and a 4, 5, 6.
Toes pointed always.

The only kind of strict I'll accept,
The rush of being on the stage.
Dancing, no, levitating,
Levitating so gracefully,
I could swear I was a spirit.
I doubt the audience could even see me;
Ghost of the theatre,
Should be my name.

The burst of cheers and applause,
That's what brings me back to earth.
It reminds me of heaven,
Though I wouldn't be able to tell you which.
Would it matter?
The feeling of being real and not,
Depends how hope and heaven relates for you.
For me,
The hell of the pain in my feet,
The humiliation of stupid costumes,
That's my hope and my heaven.
Unholy heaven,
Heaven on earth.

The worst kind of agony

Why do you put me through this pain,
Just let me hold you.
I will serve you,
Love you,
Do as you say
I will be your slave.

I'm hurting,
Trying,
Begging,
Longing.
Why don't you reciprocate?

You're breaking me.
Is this what you intend to do?
Are you being ignorant,
Are you ignoring me?

Why is it always that I have to make the first move?
Is it because I'm the only one who holds our love?
You're hurting me,
hunting me,
Forcing me to be your innocent prey.

Please release me from this grip you have me on,
I cannot bear this any longer.
You're breaking me,
Are you aware of this?

Please.
I truly beg,
What can I make of my life if my every thought is about you.
Let me be at peace,
At least give me peace of mind.

My clueless flame

I so very long for you,
I dream of bumping into you purely to be gifted with a glimpse of your beauty,
Inner and outer alike.

I yearn for your warmth,
I hope of running into you,
so I can hear your ear affectionate voice,
A perfect remedy for any nodus.

I utterly crave our conversations,
I ache to let your needle and thread akin assertiveness mend my heart,
Then embroider it effortlessly,
making it warmer and withal tender than ever before.

Hooked on doubt

I feel you could compare anything to life,
Even the most arbitrary things.
Take fishing as an example;
Sitting... waiting...
It's a simple yet adversely tedious thing,
Anticipating an opportunity to strike.
It could be a matter of minutes or hours,
But if you prove not fully prepared,
That opportunity disappears in a matter of seconds.

Some may choose to miss the opportunity,
because they believe it'll arise again.
Or as they have confidence in the fact that it's not the right timing,
But there proves hesitation to be a cruel occurrence.
They missed their chance.
Whether that's due to their lack of self trust,
Miscalculation or even self confidence.
Their chance suddenly wasn't a chance,
It became a missed opportunity.

Pushing people away

Don't be so pessimistic.

You always say I'm pessimistic but how could I not be with the way this world treats people?

That is a pessimistic viewpoint.

And you're such an optimist?

Yes this world treats people like shit but there are good times, you can't have good times without bad otherwise it'd just be unbalanced.

I guess, But then why do I always feel broken? Trapped with no way out, just me and walls of troubles and anxiety to throw myself onto.

Well I don't know.. And I-

Tell me, why after all the help I've received am I still like this? I hate how fragile I am, even breathing could knock myself over.

We can get you help.

Help? I'm sick of your so called 'help', this is the beginning of the end, doomsday.

You always exaggerate so much.

I say what I feel, you're lucky enough to get that privilege alone so be grateful.

Whatever.

That's what i thought, forget about me like everyone has.

Tints of red

If walls could talk,
They'd challenge my favourite colour,
being red.
They would say they know it's blue,
Due to the colour spilling from you.
If anything over that then brown,
But it's too predictable to favour the colour of your eyes.

I insist,
Red is most cherished.
The reason being,
Most, if not all acts of passion,
are coloured red.

The flash of red light,
When you're knocked unconscious,
After challenging a belief.
The fireworks,
Coloured crimson,
That burst surrounding two lovers embrace.

The maroon pool,
Draining from the deceased.
The scarlet of the tempting lingerie and lips,
Of a seductress.

Whether it's a slow burn,
or a flash on the horizon,
As if someone were to return from the dead.
Passion is my favourite colour,
Not brown,
not blue,
But red.

What are people?

Picked pips,
thrown into a burlap sack.
Distributed,
grown by each lonely, willing person.
A chip, inserted into a computer,
The data on it leading to a world of advanced advantages.

Emotions are so fragile,
I should break them,
They beat me to it.

Humans are similar,
So tedious to care for,
Mind, we aren't complied to.

People are possessions,
Dreadful, deceiving, decaying possessions.
Seeds derived from the fruit of life.
Drained seeds, deprived of sunlight,
water and oxygen,
Yet are still living.
Not how they'd hope, though.

My unkept diary

<u>April 26th 3:00pm</u>

I enjoyed our conversation,
You seem so down to earth.
You love all the things that I do,
But don't worry,
This won't become anything more.

<u>May 4th 9:28am</u>

I haven't stopped telling my friends about you,
What is there to even like?
Your stupid smile,
The way you laugh,
How your eyes light up when you're talking about something you love...
Shit.

<u>May 22nd 11:49am</u>

You're an inside joke now,
At least you're not simply a joke,
Not to me anyway.
I think about you daily,
Act on it more so.

<u>June 12th 7:26pm</u>

You said 'hi' to me today,
You must love me.
You acknowledged me,
Therefore I'll now kneel before you,
Your wish is my command.

August 4th 4:18am

I can't sleep,
All I can think about is you,
You haven't texted me in a month.
I want to run away from you,
But you leave the bitter scent of you,
With every thought.

August 13th 7:30am

Still no text,
Fuck.
What did I do wrong?
Why don't you love me,
Please,
I so crave you.

August 29th 1:02am

Kiss me in the clouds,
You may as well be a stranger to me.
I know about you,
I know what car you have,
Your licence plate.
Where you live,
Your pets names.
What you order at a restaurant,
Your tendencies to like a schedule.
Call me a stalker all you want,
You're the one that walked away with my heart.
I can't live without you, my love.

<u>8th oct 1:05pm</u>

I didn't think you'd show,
Does this mean you love me?
Shame,
You could've saved a life.

Contending with nodi

Problems
Aware,
Combined with anxiety
Terrifying.
Relying
On people
To be the answer
Yet,
They prove:
To just be another question.

Life where there's not

I walk daily through a graveyard,
not for mourning or for visiting,
for I have no one I consider family there.
I go there with the purpose of placing a flower,
atop a new resting place every day,
one that doesn't have any kind of fresh life representing beauty sitting
there beforehand.
As, although I have no one considered family staying there,
a headstone with a soul beneath it,
one that tells its own unique story,
with no reminiscence of life around to tell such a story,
no family of their own marking that life with a flower,
should always be considered a friend.

Never alone in our being alone

A day to myself,
One that I didn't know I needed.
A day for me,
For things I like to do.
A day to breathe,
But for love, I still pleaded.
A day to myself,
Yet all I can think about is you.

I've read and I've shopped,
I've written till I've dropped.
My energy draining from me,
Despite the leisure I've had.
Still,
the fact I've not stopped thinking of you hasn't left me much egad.

Commonly you on my mind leaves me feeling fairly alone,
Constantly desperate and unrequited,
beaten and overthrown.
Yet today of all days I strangely find,
that the simple thought of you springing to my mind,
leaves me smiling and thinking the stars may have finally aligned.

A day to myself that has caused me to discover a few things,
And I realise this ending may sound entirely sappy.
As much as I love the passion longing for you brings,
I think I've ultimately realised,
I don't need you to be happy.

Love me in life

Looming swampish
clouds, Turned
Depressingly leaking.

Dirt, squelching
Under soles.
The very
dirt, To adapt,
Spirit and soul.

Attending members,
Black cloth holding
Tears split.

A face, with
An O for
A mouth, one
That shares a name.

A face and
Grave, coincidentally
Mirroring mine.

Shock for
Attendance.
Being fulfilled,
By great sums.

I choose to love you

I open the door with the golden handle,
The one that leads to your study which was strictly off limits.
The smell of you torments me,
It hits me in the face and brings back so many memories.
I look to the corner where your shirts hang sadly,
The shoes beneath them collect dust.
I go to your desk and see the photos of us,
The time shared.
It feels utterly like a dream,
It's hard to believe you ever really existed.

It's hard to believe the world would take you away from me.
We may remain soulmates yet the lack of your touch urges me to feel
distant from your soul.
I feel as though I'm falling out of love with you,
Something that would finally put my mind at ease yet... I don't want it to
happen.

The thoughts I get involving you, are my happiness.
They're what make even the worst of days full of elation.
I know I should want to be able to move on but I can't,
I can't bring myself to do that.
I don't want you... but I need you.

The calm before the storm

I love thunderstorms,
I love how something so formidable can be so peaceful.
Like a friendly giant,
One that refuses to understand you,
Until you understand it.

Raindrops tapping the window panes,
Inky and gloomy clouds filling the sky.
Some people hiding under their blankets;
Intimated and alarmed.
Others who take the chance to grab a book and some candles,
To sit upon the window ledge and relax.

My favourite part, though,
would have to be the calm before the storm.
The tranquillity,
the colour saturated sky.
The duplicity of something being so divine one minute then abandoning
all hope and attraction for the purpose of trickery the next.
Like a siren,
The seductress famous for luring you in with beauty and heavenly
lullabies,
Then captures you in its raging fatalistic aura.

Boredom

Watching the clock make its vigorous ticking sound,
Tick, tick, tick
Watching the clock; making every second seem like an eternity.
Tick, tick, tick
What happens if the clock breaks,
no more clicking,
no more ticking,
just silence...

Boredom is a terrible master
Yet when you're offered a substitute,
Boredom seems to become an enjoyable moment.
Silence and peace,
Rather than ennui and apathy.

How do you fix boredom?
It's as if you're too energetic to not do anything,
but on the contrary, too indolent to do anything else.
It's a cruel eventuality,
One that is dreaded,
yet uncomfortably welcomed.

Is this living?

We breathe,
We reproduce,
We die,
We entertain.

Breathing is so obnoxious,
Stealing the air from others;
How selfish.
You may as well steal it straight from their lungs,
You taker of life.

Lust is a repulsive thing.
Most living organisms are lustful,
They quench togetherness;
Unbecoming.
We desire companionship and pleasure;
Unseemly.

Death,
The unavoidable fate,
The cruel actuality of time;
perpetual.
We stand no chance against kismet,
Death is arguably the thing that affects us most.
Ultimately damaging.

Yet each of these things to us are entertainment.
We sit endlessly viewing other people's lives,
Whether that's via the media,
publication or experience with people that surround us.
We've made amusement out of each other;
Disenchanting,
Disheartening,
Depressing.

Ouroboros

Mortality has fucked me over,
I'm sick of waiting for prince charming,
Tired of not breathing until **he** looks in my direction.

This punishment is unnecessary,
I have only the love in my heart to blame,
Not the stupidity in my head.

I don't blame myself,
I don't blame **him**.
The problem has fabricated itself,
But what vexes me is that **he** is the only solution.

Places that don't have access to water,
I could drown with my tears.
Even the deaf could hear my wails,
The blind to see my desperation.

A waste of energy,
Too many lost causes of dropped weeping.
Frustrating,
Knowing what's wrong but not being able to concern anyone.
As you know that a simple slip up of the silver tongue,
Has the power of a thousand falling suns.

False beauty

The buzz of a bee is a peaceful yet damaging sound,
A beautiful creature that appears heavenly,
until it takes up the opportunity to mark you with its predatorial sting.

Romeo's soliloquy

Rising to the sight of the travelling lamp can not compareth to rising to
the sight of thee,
The rival of Aphrodite.
Mine own quite quaint dove,
mine own peaceful love.

I gaze thee catch but a wink,
thou art soundeth, quiet.
still thee maketh thy presence known regardless,
using thy beauty.

I desire to nev'r waketh thee from thy slumb'r,
mine own hypnos,
mine own sleeping enchantress.
rest, ladybird,
i desire you're dreaming a dreameth w'rth a thousand.

The sapphire in my eyes

Blood looks the same,
no matter who it spills from.
Bone stays white and pure,
Regardless of the staining ichor surrounding.

We all share the same faith,
Not christianity or hinduism,
Nor Judaism or buddhism.
I speak of the faith we give to ourselves.

We give faith to life,
As well as to our society.
We take faith from life,
As some whose perceptions are tainted by lucifer,
See it fit to do so.

We're all due the same gift,
The chance to bleed and cry,
To mourn and to die.
We are devotedly fulfilled of that worry,
And greatly so.

Those who we regard as sinners,
Do not possess thick sinking blood,
Or virtuous virgin bone.
How could they,
When for them,
To hold a soul means the opportunity to confiscate one.

Muse

To some it's a person,
A cherished loved one.
To others it may be music,
A beat of a heart,
that soulfully sounds like a drum.
Or maybe it's an art,
Although no more finite to just the one.
Some may never find their muse,
They may search and find none.
Stranded with an unfinished symphony,
that will never be sung.

Pick your poison

Drink until you're drunk,
Then drink some more.
Willingly pour that liquid poison,
Aware of its effects,
Knowing of the hours you'll spend on the bathroom floor.

Why do you do it?
Is it a release,
Or a distraction.
Is it for the few hours of dangerous happiness,
Or is it to momentarily forget.

The addiction that you believe can be most controlled,
The one that goes well in a wine glass with a meal.
The addiction that comes tailored to your taste,
The one that makes you unaware and uncaring of the people around you.
The poison that is friendly until it inevitably fires.

A museums silhouette

A person is like a work of art,
Each unique,
Each tells a story.

Being a display does prove to have its lows,
though, as well as highs.
Everyone has their own description of what art is,
Some people believe their meaning is the only correct one,
(which usually reflects on their own "masterpiece")

Some works of art,
People find confusing or misleading.
People will either show this opinion by embracing it,
or becoming angered and rejecting it.
No inbetween.

Art can be any form or colour,
Can portray any message or struggle.
A person's creativity always has a deeper meaning,
Some people may seek that meaning and never find it.
Others find it but never cherish it.

A simple message, really,
Art is art, art is emotion.
It's tragedy, loss,
Simple yet different.

Art is a rose that has found itself blossoming in winter,
It is a miracle and a burden.
It is a story,
But most importantly:

Art
   Is
      Life.

Remedy for a broken heart

Out the window is where I stare,
Too many words flying through the air.
No matter how many of them are said,
none of them I hear.
It upsets and confuses me,
this headache of despair.

What you do to me is entirely unfair,
You're cruel like a bitter cold night,
biting and bare.
Your presence distances me from the safety of this world,
yet makes me feel uncomfortably aware.

The wealth of emotions you provide me with makes me feel like an heir,
Whilst forcing me into rags of anguished wear and tear.
You make me worship a god I don't believe in with my desperate prayers.
Just love me all ready, my satisfactions affair.

Reliable wounds

I thought you would be the one to fix me.

Hear me,
See me,
Admire me,
Mirthfully.

Love me,
Trust me,
Embrace me,
Blissfully.

Distance me,
Hurt me,
Hate me,
Ruthfully.

Yet you've helped to break me.

An empty souvenir

The halls echo my name,
As I elapse by,
alike the months since I've been forgotten.
There are no pictures of me decorated,
Due to never achieving anything worth framing.

The background is my refuge.
A sanctuary I share with no one but a serpent and a mirror.
Often though,
I find when I look around,
The brother of Nāḥāš had abandoned me.

What may have been misinterpreted is my living,
You may not actually be able to call this 'living'.
Regardless,
my suit of smiles is still intact,
Comparable to the fresh air still being inspired and inhaled.

I live for nothing,
but a love that hates
and a life that is killing me.
A ghost I am not,
But a lost spirit.

We have but a single face

"Are you okay?",
I hear from behind my mask of hands.
No answer,
Silence is definitely necessary.

Telling you what worries me is as pointless as watering the garden just
before it rains.

I already waste my time,
indulging myself into the neverending cat and mouse romance I've made
my life,
Why waste my breath too?

It's not like you would understand the pain of ripping a rose by the
thorns anyway.

"No",
Is the answer to your formally asked question.
But once again I present myself as 'Loki',
God of trickery.
"I'm fine, Thank you!".

A rush of emotions

I don't trust people,
I don't usually trust people,
Yet you managed to gain my trust in a matter of seconds.

How?
How have you managed to break down my barriers so easily?
Please speak.
Tell me, I need to know how to enforce my walls.

Not as I don't want people coming in,
It just seems I'm the only one protecting me.
You've entered my heart too swiftly.
I don't want you to leave,
I just want to be safe.

In the heat of the moment

I'll continue playing with you,
Like a harp made of heat.
Strumming your throbbing bud,
To hear your melodic moans.

The ardour trapped between our bodies,
Reminding me of fire you make burn inside of myself.
The one that is impossible to put out,
Even using the puddles of love we leave.

I see you as a dragon,
A fire breather, a passion infuser.
I know you as the bonfire that looks so tempting,
I'd always dare to dip my hand into the pool of flames for the pleasure of
the burn.
I imagine you as a star,
That ignited ball ablaze.
Always noticing,
Yet never being able to reach my hand far enough to grasp onto the idea.
The idea of you not being you,
But him.

Captured by time

Not a day goes by where I don't miss you,
I weep soulfully into a tear soaked tissue,
Oh, what I would give to tenderly kiss you.
But alas the moments we shared are not valid for woeful renew.

"Sweeping you off your feet"
A phrase that references falling in love,
Well to me it's not just a phrase,
It's an action, I want to watch you fly like a dove.

I would kill to see you in a flowing dress,
One that looks like a waterfall.
I'd stare into those Crystal like eyes,
Those pupils that are fragile, Small.

I'd spin you around the ballroom,
Make you feel as if you were floating.
Watch you fly around with joy painted on your face,
Your smile doing all the emoting.

A shame that now as memories fade,
And stage like echos are done being played
I struggle to recall those fragile eyes,
I can't seem to relive your emoting smile.
I feel as though time has come to collect those memories that were
undoubtedly worthwhile.

I try to remember all of those sunny days,
Those beautiful moments weren't just a phase.
I will love you forever,
that feeling stays.
I remember you by placing bouquets,
by looking into the sun's gaze and feeling all the golden rays.
My heart's desire, you do amaze.
My one promised as life replays,
we'll find each other, love has its ways.

Your silver is my gold

When i asked God for riches,
I meant an abundance of gold.
I wished upon a genie,
For everlasting wealth,
I received a heart that was cold.

When i wished upon a star,
The one with brightness most bold.
I wanted to use it to buy happiness,
Yet now mine is all sold.

Every simple breath of yours you take,
Seems now they should withhold.
When i asked God for riches,
I didn't assume a love uncontrolled.

Comforting emptiness

Your kisses make me melt,
I wish they could do more.
I feel so safe in your arms,
But it's the solitary place I do,
So our cuddles are often tear soaked.

I'm able to hold the waterfall in,
But when I fall into your arms,
The dam starts to crack.
I know nothing of stability,
When it comes to you.

Tears are supposedly salty,
But they taste like home with you.
Strange, as I have no home to speak of,
Just walls strengthened by disputes.
Still, my eyes favour the shelter of your shoulders.
The smell of your affection,
The fraught warmth of your hue.

<u>Dreaming</u>

What is sleep if not a vessel to something greater?
A way of aiding your mind to create a world of endless possibilities.
What is a dream if not an escape,
A way of reaching what you desire most.
After all the beauty of dreaming is ethereal,
Infatuating and passionate like a blood soaked rose.

A cruel puppeteer

This poem isn't a poem,
Because I've ran out of words to say to you.
I could sit here until the sun refuses to rise,
Working the cogs of my mind so they don't have a chance to rust.
But you've now taken everything,
Even my willingness to not give up.

I'd gladly be dragged to hell by you,
If it meant I got to hold your hand.
You've made that seem like a pleasure now,
A chance I'll never get.
You are a dagger to me,
The only difference:
you make me feel like I'd kill to bleed.

My tired mind is no competitor,
to the string around your finger that you're holding me on.
This poem isn't a poem,
Just a list I wish I'd have the nerve to say to you.

Love escalates

There's nothing better than love,
Two souls finally connected.
Their conscious loving minds at work,
Warming each other with every glance.
Fighting through everything together like the team they are,
Although momentarily the disputes are between the team mates,
Still, getting through them as always.
Strength and uniqueness in their love,
Well, in this bond they call, 'love'.
"Do I look fat in this dress"?,
Idiotic nerve, careful bravery,
"a little".
You fool, you fiend, are you trying to ruin this?
"Out. Now. I want you OUT."
"I didn't mean to sleep with him!"
Maybe it was jealousy,
 a hunch of a mistress of his own.
Maybe even revenge,
Though I'd say excuse.
You shouldn't need excuse to be happy.
There's nothing better than love, yes,
But there's nothing worse than it either.

Seventh heaven

Ecstasy comes at a high cost, Release at a higher.
Compared to the feeling of the perfect weather for the beach,
compared to running through a field of flowers feeling free.
The pleasure companionship gives you is everything.
More euphoric,
more absolute,
more freeing.
A rare but giving feeling of elation that lingers.
Ignorant bliss if you will.

Paper roses

I wouldn't mind,
To die tonight.
Peacefully in my sleep,
All but me and your heart.
For we would go quietly,
But of course painfully,
There's no peace in pain.

I wouldn't want to wake you,
That's why I'll be silent.
All I need is the nest of golden feathers,
Silent promises,
To keep me content.

I'm comfortable with the suffering,
As long as it's for you,
As long as it's not with.
Dying would be a pleasure in any case,
But dying to the softness of your skin,
The moisture of your gentle, healing tears,
Is more than I could ever hope.

An ode to conflict

A rulership,
Dictation.
Disagreement,
Departure.
Fleeing,
Terrified?
Envy,
War,
Loss.

Loss for the brave ones who dared to go against the established,
Gain for those who sit upon their high horse.
A land that needed a ruler,
Turned to an army, fighting the fled.
In a war it's hard to decide who is truly more assured,
Or better so, frightened.
A peaceful protest gone haywire,
A community that decided to split.
A fight among men that lead to betrayal,
Or even worse, death.

A ruler ship, one voted for by fellow lowlifes.
Dictation, the monarch's dominion,
written for adherents to adhere to.
Disagreement, followers' hesitance.
Departure, their soon followed rebellion.
Fleeing, a future soon to be reached,
but only later to be decided whether it was worth it.
Terrified, and every right to be,
yet exhilarated, brave.
Envy, the constraining feeling of wanting it more now knowing you can't
have it.
War, deciding to take what you believe to be rightfully yours.
Loss, for there is loss in every battle,
as needless as it is.

An abolished aurora borealis

Do you ever just feel,
Well,
Do you ever not?
The nothingness of emotions seeping through me,
The carelessness of tears and smiles.
I throw them away like they're nothing to me,
Because that is all they are, nothing.

I fear that's all they ever will be,
"What are you feeling today?",
I'm asked,
How am I supposed to know?
Genuinely,
Please give me access to myself,
My mind is a prisoner.

"What's wrong?",
I don't know.
I'm so useless,
Why don't I know the cause of this flood in my head?
I'm not here, i'm never here,
Just like how I never know.

Is there an end?

Is there an end,
To the sky swollen rainbow.
Is there an end,
To my ever growing pain.
Is there an end,
To the sun's radiation.
Is there an end,
To the heavy, frightful rain.

A limit to the height,
Of a towering skyscraper,
For it truly scrapes the sky.
Build something too eagerly,
It crashes back down to the earth.
Like a bird,
One so beautiful,
Yet can't fly.

Is there an end,
To our pit of despair,
That we lay thinking about at night.
Is there an end,
To life after life,
Do our souls finally give up the fight?

I choose to love you

I open the door with the golden handle,
The one that leads to your study which was strictly off limits.
The smell of you torments me,
It hits me in the face bring back so many memories.
I look to the corner where your shirts hang sadly,
The shoes beneath them collecting dust.
I go to your desk and see the photos of us,
The time shared;
It feels utterly like a dream,
It's hard to believe you ever really existed.

It's hard to believe the world would take you away from me.
We may remain soulmates yet the lack of your touch urges me to feel
distant from your soul.
I feel as though I'm falling out of love with you,
Something that would finally put my mind at ease yet... I don't want it to
happen.

The thoughts I get involving you, are my happiness.
They're what make even the worst of days full of elation.
I know I should want to be able to move on but I can't,
I can't bring myself to do that.
I don't want you... but I need you.

Manipulation or paranoia?

Bury your head in my chest,
Like you would a newly passed loved one in an eternal pit of darkness.
Feel yourself sink into me,
As if you were drowning with no way to save yourself.
Melt into me and combine with me,
Embody a forest fire, one that's wide spread and seemingly impossible to tame.
Be me,
Adapt all the behaviours I have, no matter the seeping toxicity.
Marry me,
Wear that glorified handcuff of love that makes you a sinner to remove.

Be prepared to take all blame.
This was your choice wasn't it?
Was it not what you wanted?
This is all your fault.
No wonder we're not happy.
You've ruined my life,
Due to recklessness of your own.
I want you gone but you're wrong if you think I'll be the first to go.
You simple pawn,
My puppet on a string.
death do us part.

The plot thickens

Addressed to whoever is writing my story.

The cast right now is better than it was a few chapters ago, they're cheerier.
In my opinion, keep the love interest, the fans may not love him but this is my book, not theirs.
Don't boot any characters, please, the plot line is thick enough, I'm going through enough.
Speaking of which,
you're a writer, a creator,
So why are you acting more like the devil than a god?
You must be a genius writer,
To be able to make someone else the main character in my book.
You make me feel like the world revolves around me,
in the very worst of times.
You make it so my world collapses,
At the very best.
I say all this in hopes of you deciding I actually do get a say,
But as always, I'll continue writing,
Until I desperately get my way.

Sun and moon

The sun shone so bright,
How could the moon resist?
The sun's beauty and grace,
Compared to the moon's misery and murk.
The moon decided that he wanted a light shone onto his life,
The sun decided the moons darkness was endearing and shy,
They both decided to love, till they die.

A few years on,
Handfuls of eclipses.
Delicate kisses and touches,
As many as they could secure.
The sun decided one day,
To gift the moon a ray of gold.
One to devotionally hug a finger,
To show a bond, one of promise.

The moon then wept Tears,
Made of stardust,
but these were not happy tears,
they were ones of despair.
For the moon could not accept the suns proposal,
as the sun would simply burst with happiness.
Neither could the moon decline,
The sun would darken with a shroud of sorrow.
So the moon answered with an unsure one,
The moon said "I don't know".

Earth was Ofcourse sad,
As she offered Mother Nature as the flower girl.
Mars to be the blush,
on the bride's cheeks and lips alike.
To this day,
Saturn holds the rings.
To the day after,
They fade a little more.

So when we look,
Up to the sky,
And a fiery hell is falling upon us.
Be joyous, don't fret,
As love kills for a chance.
Just be happy the moon finally said yes.

Death can't coexist

I hope death is sweet,
I hope it's salty,
I hope it's all I imagine it to be,
I hope it's everything and nothing,
Light and heavy.

I hope death is kind to me,
I hope it takes me gently.
Like a baby abandoned at a doorstep,
I hope I'm accepted and unaware of the tragedy I faced beforehand.

I hope death loves life,
I hope he feels sympathy.
I hope he's as enlivened to meet me,
As I am to meet him.
I want death to be lenient,
I want him to be open handed.
With that open hand to take me soulfully,
In spite of the lack of soul.

The time for horror

As august falls,
So do I,
Under the weight of the stunning,
Fire coloured leaves.

The smell of pumpkin spice,
The feel of gorgeous warm sweaters,
What isn't there to love about autumn?
Its miserable trees,
Stripped bare of leaves,
Jealous of how beautiful they've become,
Without the home the tree thought they so needed.

Carving pumpkins,
As i wish to carve myself,
I guess it just has a prettier outcome,
Yet even I'd disagree with myself there.

Halloween,
would have to be my favourite october festivity.
I get to dress up frightening,
I could dress as my emotions this year,
It would be fitting.

The movies halloween brings i love too,
As many people do.
Sad that majority of them watch their favourite horrors alone,
With no one but a pillow to hide behind,
At Least it makes being alone a little scarier.

Did you know that black cats,
Face complete increased danger during october.
Reason being,
they're supposedly used for rituals.
How dare we say,
that they're the ones who bring back luck.

Then october comes to an end,
People put up their christmas trees
Whilst their children are left with a bag of sweets and treats.
Given to them by strangers,
Which will be sure to make them feel self conscious,
After eating it all as a solution to a breakdown.
Oh, how I love autumn.

Ol' Saint Nick

Ol' Saint Nick,
We know who he is,
He knows us more.
See's us when were sleeping,
Knows when were awake,
Thinks we should believe in him,
Or our lives will be at stake.
The one who brings us gifts,
The very same with coal,
If you've been naughty then you'll be punished,
But gifted if you have a matching soul.
Kind and cheery santa clause,
Knows just want we want,
Knows our addresses too,
Forces it upon us even if we don't.
Frightening Father christmas,
The one who gave birth to snow,
I hope i can keep some things,
That he'll never get to know.

Kisses doused in red

Kiss me on top of the sand,
On the beach where we shared our first.
Flick me a smirk like smile,
While quenching my very desperate thirst.

Care for me in sickness and health,
Tend to my ever growing ail.
Waste all your precious moments,
You with me,
Whilst your mates share happiness of ale.

Turn me cold blooded, a killer,
Your heart murdered and ate.
My love for you standing eternity,
Like an infinite figure of eight.

Thick red spilt everywhere,
So the clothes now have to dye.
But no matter how many people do,
Our love will never die.

What is life worth?

The beaches you won't get to trek,
The seas longing to engulf you.
The sights you'll get to see,
The family to share the view.

The clouds you'll fail to taste,
The loss of your sugar sweet breath.
The Happiness you'll bring to others,
The sadness in the absence of death.

The greed coming to haunt you,
The haunting you'll do yourself.
The Blood that won't get to spill,
The gift of sunrise in health.

7 deadly sins

What doesn't kill you,
makes you stronger.
But what will plague you,
Are the sins in the dearth of death.

Pride, Lucifer,
Ones overwhelming vainglory,
The mockery in your cockiness.
Please take pride in yourself,
As you are who you are.
But beware you're not taken,
By wealth of ego and amour propre.

Greed, Mammon,
You thief of covetousness,
Fill yourself with sins as well as your own,
Though never becoming full.
It's never enough for you,
The mountains of gold.
The meals at your table,
The walls that surround.

Lust, Asmodeous,
Desire filling you,
Disgusting illicit fool.
Deviant of sexual fantisies,
Riddling your mind with unrestrained craving.
Be pure and lock your heart,
For your mind is already poisoned.

Envy, Beelzebub,
Be happy with what you have,
For some have much less.
Don't chase after designer wants,
Instead be thankful for God's gift.
Thank him for what he's given,
Thank him for what he's not.

Gluttony, Belphegor,
Shove it down your throat,
You pig,
Drink until you can't anymore.
Plug your body with excessive death,
The phrase is "pick your poison",
For good reason.
Douse your lining with happiness,
Pour so much it becomes your core.

Wrath, Sathanas,
You're holding a grudge,
Angry at the air for being thin.
Why let rage take over your body,
Spin out of control,
from the heat of the moment.
Be patient,
Breath deep,
You won't get that pleasure much longer.

Sloth, Abadon,
Like pulling the plug from a bath,
One that you thoroughly enjoyed.
Why do anything at all,
When happiness comes from home.
Your bed warms you more,
Then the thought of eating or breathing.
So suffocate in your pillows and self pity,
Too lazy to gasp for air.

Your sin will follow your soul,
No matter how many times you make up.
Because the demons accept your fate,
As soon as your first word is the end.
For no compassion falls upon lucifer.

The eye of a hurricane

We've upset god,
So we're receiving what he thinks is punishment.
My heart drops every time the lighting makes itself known,
But that is a pleasure above anything, being frightened by Thor.
Thunder trapped in clouds,
Bouncing around the walls of beauty,
Then spitting a force of pure power.
Trees struck down with fire,
Fogs passion crashing down to earth.
The flag of raging electricity,
Mithering the air,
Smothering the earth's body.
I like how it lights the sky,
Brighter than day could ever get to be,
It shows we can always be more,
With a little temper and crucifixion.

Heaven in the waves

The waves crashing against each other,
In such an aggressive yet polite way.
The habitat that it holds is more than just the beauty of wildlife,
It's the model of mannerisms.
The warmed sand underneath you,
Falling out of your grasp like material heaven.
When the perfect position is found,
We float on the water like clouds under our wings.
Water becoming as light as air,
Holding our worries as well as our bodies.
For there's something special in the sea,
That holds our attention and breath,
The meaning of our liveliness.

The final stretch

Are you disappointed,
Is this not what you'd thought it'd be.
Does it not fit the perfect imagine in your mind,
The one impossible to match.
Have you given up faith in me?
Left me as soon as the air became thick,
It started suffocating me.
I have a headache,
Punching the walls of my mind,
I may as well hit my head against a steel door.
Have I failed you,
The incomplete thought in my heart,
Not enough for you.
I get the starving feeling,
That life has given you,
But if you think you'll ever be truly full,
You're going to become extremely disappointed.
Never enough for you,
Shovelling literacy in your face,
Just to feel something.
I hope you are dissatisfied,
It's better than having a black hole,
Where your emotions should lay.

Serving the ever vacant earth

Is this what falling out of love feels like?
A deer,
before the haunting vision of the headlights.
A map,
With all locations crossed out.
A life,
One that's accomplished and completed.

Do I get to be normal again?
Will there ever even be a 'normal',
That I get to return to.
Do I get to finally act my age,
Vaping, drinking, partying.
Not hiding in the cave of pillows,
Soaking them with a drug only love can supply.

I never saw our love as a thing,
Able to fall out of.
Then again,
Maybe my mind is continuing to taunt itself.
Playing the sort of tricks you would on a sibling.
I'd believe if you told,
That I'm falling out of love.
But 'normal' isn't a title I can hold.

About the author

My name is Cody Zatac, I'm 16 years old and over the last year, my life has turned around. I've always been loud and confident, I've always enjoyed activities such as singing or acting, painting and crafting, though I would never have considered myself a writer. I was never one to find peace in pages of books. In 2021 I was diagnosed with depression after years of struggling, then about 9 months ago (feb 2022) I was finally prescribed antidepressants and I really feel that's what kicked off the change in my life. I was constantly tired and couldn't be bothered with even getting out of bed, which is a feeling I'm sure you'd have experienced before. I filled my life with as much colour as I could, I would constantly be painting or decorating, collecting things I love, like crystals and earrings, the most vibrant and unique I could find. I really felt like I did those things in an attempt to try and cheer myself up. I drowned myself in things I enjoyed in order to feel something, though that something was rarely ever happiness. Since starting medication I'm really enjoying the simple things in life, especially words. I started with a makeover for my room. There would be my paintings and drawings covering the walls as I wanted to be proud of myself, I thought it would make me see that I am useful and that I am worth something. Pictures of my favourite tv shows plastered the walls too, as well as plushies drowning the floors. I kept all the paintings of course, all but two went into draws, I kept up the simple ones, one of which I believe remains my best work. My teal walls now stand a dark brown and the depressing peeling wallpaper is now one that's brand new and patterned with books. It seems a lot calmer now, more aesthetic and comforting. One of the first things that changed was my taste in music, i've always loved musicals and loud show tune type songs and I of course still do, but if I had to choose a favourite type of music it would be classical, my favourite piece would have to be debussys 'Clair de lune', i find it so peaceful. With poetry I feel the first real step into it was really a butterfly effect, caused by agreeing to watch 'pirates of the caribbean - the curse of the black pearl' with my dad and brother as I'd been wanting to watch that film series in any case. After watching it, I thought it was an alright movie - mediocre - but had the urge to watch it again a few weeks later (I have now watched each film in that series about 20 times).

What stood out to me the second time around though was the actor for 'Captain Hector Barbossa' aka. Geoffrey rush (my now favourite actor, who i wrote to and received a signed photograph back!). From there I watched every film I could find with any type of appearance from him, the first and most life changing for me being 'Quills' . Now I know that may seem weird if you are aware of what Quills is about, but it is the only movie I've ever truly cried at. Something shifted in me after watching that film, it inspired me, so much so it only took an hour to decide to do an art project on 'Marquis De Sade', the film's protagonist (perhaps even the antagonist). I spent a month on that art project and from it I gained pride and self confidence (about time). The book thief was the close second. I loved the message of that film, so much so I decided to buy the book when I saw it in a shop a week later. This book opened the chance of conversation with a teacher I favoured in the school, so of course I took that chance. From then our conversations grew and varied but to me that was really my first step into poetry. Probably another week after that was my dad's birthday where 'provoking speech' was born, of course it wasn't going to be amazing or polished, it was my first poem, but it was **mine**. I was so very proud of it, and to think now I've written 60. I showed that poem to my new english teacher (as id moved up a set due to very weird circumstances, but it was totally worth it) and to the teacher I'd been speaking to, I mean it was only fit to do so, he has been an english teacher for years and i wanted his opinion. It felt so homely to me to write that poem, so i didnt stop. I started posting my poems to an instagram account @Passion_In_Poetry_ is what i called it, i was then asked to join a group of writers who encourage each other and help spread each other's poems. This is becoming very much like an autobiography now and I don't want to blabble on too much so I'll stop myself but yes, that was the beginning of my love of poetry.

x - my cat Mozart sat on my laptop and typed this 'x' so I felt it should stay in honour of him.

This book holds the first 50 poems I've ever written. Poetry has become such an apparent thing in my life in the last year and has helped me through bad days and breakdowns. To me, poetry is an escape, somewhere I can run away to whenever I please. I often find myself not being able to find the words to explain what i'm feeling but as soon as pen hits paper words spill. Most poems in this book are themed around unrequited love. I've always found unrequited love the easiest to write about. As I've always said, it's something that I feel speaks the most words, holds the most exposed emotions and has the most struggle. I hope you enjoy reading this gateway to my emotions, if any. I lay my mind bare for you to discover.

Printed in Great Britain
by Amazon